Finding You, Little One

By Carly Eccles Sheaffer
Illustrated by AJ Eccles

Little Sister Books
Golden Bridges Publishing
www.goldenbridgespublishing.com

Published in the United States by Little Sister Books, an imprint of Golden Bridges Publishing 2024

Copyright © 2024 by Carly Eccles Sheaffer

All rights reserved.

No part of this book may be reproduced in any form or by any electronic or mechanical means, including information storage and retrieval systems, without written permission from the author, except for the use of brief quotations in a book review.

Library of Congress Control Number: 2024947890
ISBN (Print): 979-8-9907356-2-0
ISBN (ebook): 979-8-9907356-3-7

Finding You, Little One

Remembering our little one:

_____

For Abram,
tiny but mighty,
our star in the sky.
You are loved, sweet boy.
So loved.
All my heart,
Mama

When we miss you, little baby,
When our hearts feel like they broke,
Little One, we find your spirit
Everywhere our family looks.

Knowing you are with us,
That your memory is so real,
We find you within our story,
Helping our hearts to heal.

Nestled in the nooks of moments,
Whispering in the wind…
There's magic that knows your spirit is here,
Rippling 'round every bend.

So, Little One,
We'll find you.

We'll find you in the roses,
Soft petals curled in just so,
And the small ones nodding,
Not yet bloomed....

Oh, the ways that grace can grow.

We'll find you in the smell of evergreen,
breathing in winter joy and healing.

Between the branches and homemade treasures you'll be,
Forever green and gleaming.

You'll be in gatherings around the table,
In the meals for each other shared,
In the stories,
The holding of hands,
The creak of old worn chairs.

You'll be in the loveliest of snowfalls,
Softly settling in the night air,
Every flake irreplaceably its own.

Little One, we'll find you there.

Between bike races and ball games,
Little One, there you'll be.

In the laughter, the yells,
The delight of life,
The sound of joy and family.

You'll be in the rolling mountains
Who shelter, who endure.
Those blue-green hues surrounding,
Wise and quietly sure.

We'll find you
In the salty ocean wind,
Across the waters and ebbing tides,
Peace where the mighty sea
Meets that open sky.

We'll find you in the stars,
Little One,
When our faces turn above.

We'll find you folded in moments of
Hopeful kindness and of love.

In every beat of our hearts,
We'll remember yours all over again.
And there, in that steady
Ba-bum-ba-bum-ba-bum
You'll be, Little One, within.

For Grieving Loved Ones, A Note from the Author:

Everyone grieves differently. Losing a child through miscarriage, stillbirth, as a baby, or as a child evokes deeply intense grief. Nothing prepares you for this unimaginable goodbye.

When I was almost six months pregnant, we found out our little boy had zero percent chance of survival; he was stillborn a few weeks later. In the months following I learned

the power of grief, the waves that hit you out of nowhere, and the sharp, raw pain of missing your baby so much it hurts
that society is only just now making infant death less taboo, despite 1-4 women experiencing this similar, heartbreaking journey
that talking about our baby Abram -especially with our children- and fully feeling the impact of his short time with us was incredibly important.

As loved ones, we know: these babies are a part of our story.

Grief affects our mental and emotional selves, as well as our relationships. Parents experience depression, shock, anger, helplessness, trauma, and the loss of self. Be gentle with your soul, no matter your mourning process and expressions of grief. Siblings may also be sad, confused, or powerless when their anticipated little brother or sister is suddenly gone. Studies show that many siblings experience grief quite significantly and risk internalizing the trauma of losing a family member. They need ways to process their grief.

"Closure" is a concept that frustrates many families, as though the journey of missing their child is a finite experience. I believe it is not. Instead, we grow with our grief. This book gives space to feel, remember, love, and heal. The hole in our lives never disappears, but it changes and softens. We never stop finding our little one's spirit.

How can you grieve:

A tree, a plant, a painting, jewelry with the birthstone or initial, a wind chime, a candle, an ornament, a book, etc. Having a tangible way to remember helps ease the physical emptiness we feel, in our bellies, our arms, and our homes.

Create traditions that offer times to be intentional about your healing. Incorporate your culture, religion, or ethnic backgrounds' rituals or ceremonies. Every November 28, the day Abram was born, we hike in the mountains and leave pretty rocks overlooking the river. My kids look forward to this, which allows them to openly connect spiritually to their brother. Find your rituals that connect you to your little one's spirit.

Seek support from your village. This is a truly important part of healing while holding your little one close. Join a bereavement group, either in person and/or online; these groups help families share emotions and experiences. Connect with a therapist or counselor to help process life after loss. Lean on others. You are never alone.

Talk with your care provider, hospital, support group, counselor, or community about more resources while grieving.

Most importantly, know that your little one's spirit is with you. Always.

Milton Keynes UK
Ingram Content Group UK Ltd.
UKHW050925191124
451074UK00029B/151